Stop Yourself From Burnout

A Practical Guide To Unlock The Stress Code Plus Tips And Strategies To Regain Balance And Relieve Anxiety

By

Adam Vaney

Table of Contents

Introduction...4

    The Looming Danger................................ 6

    Burnout's Burning Effects.......................7

Chapter 1: Understanding Stress and Burnout. 9

    Stress...9

    Burnout...12

Chapter 2: Recognizing Stress.........................16

    Symptoms of Stress.......................... 16

    Identifying Sources of Stress......................... 18

    Differences Between Stress and Burnout....... 21

    Assessing Your Stress and Burnout Levels.... 26

    Self-Assessment Tools and Questionnaires... 29

Chapter 3: Combating the Stress Monster.......33

    Relaxation Techniques.................................33

    Time Management and Prioritization............. 38

    Setting Boundaries and Saying No................ 41

    Healthy Lifestyle Habits..............................43

Chapter 4: Preventing and Managing Burnout (9 Ways)..48

    Building a Support System.........................52

    Recognizing and Addressing Negative Thought Patterns...55

    Creating a Resilient Mindset..........................58

Chapter 5: Seeking Professional Help.............66

    Types of Therapy for Stress and Burnout....... 69

Conclusion... 73

Additional Resources......................................76

Bonus: Stress Diary...................................79

Introduction

Sarah had always been a high achiever. In her job as a marketing manager, she prided herself on her ability to handle multiple projects simultaneously, meet tight deadlines, and exceed expectations. But lately, something has changed.

As the demands of her job increased, Sarah found herself working longer hours, sacrificing her personal time, and neglecting her health. She was constantly stressed, overwhelmed, and exhausted, but she kept pushing herself to do more, thinking it was just a temporary phase.

Months passed, and the pressure continued to mount. Sarah's performance started to suffer, and she struggled to concentrate and stay motivated. She became irritable, withdrawn, and cynical, and her once-passionate enthusiasm for her work waned.

Despite her best efforts to keep up appearances, Sarah's colleagues began to notice her decline. They expressed concern about her well-being and urged her to take breaks and seek support, but Sarah brushed off their worries, convinced that she could handle it all on her own.

One day, Sarah hit a breaking point. She woke up feeling completely drained, unable to summon the energy to get out of bed. Tears welled up in her eyes as she realized that she couldn't continue living like this anymore. The relentless pressure had taken its toll, and she was burnt out.

With the support of her friends and family, Sarah finally acknowledged the severity of her situation and sought professional help. She took a leave of absence from work to focus on her mental and physical health, prioritizing self-care and relaxation.

During her time off, Sarah reflected on the warning signs she had ignored and the importance of setting boundaries and practicing self-compassion. She gradually regained her strength and clarity of mind, rediscovering her passion for life outside of work.

When Sarah eventually returned to her job, she did so with a renewed sense of purpose and balance. She learned to prioritize her well-being, set realistic expectations, and delegate tasks when necessary. Most importantly, she vowed never to let burnout consume her again, knowing that her health and happiness were worth far more than any professional accolade.

The Looming Danger

Stress and burnout aren't just buzzwords; they're real threats to our physical and mental wellbeing. Let's delve into the dangers they pose.

The Stressful Reality

- The American Institute of Stress reports that 80% of adults experience stress regularly especially on the job, with 32% reporting a high stress level.

- Chronic stress can manifest in various health issues, including headaches, muscle tension, insomnia, digestive problems, and a weakened immune system. The World Health Organization even recognizes stress as a contributing factor to various chronic diseases like heart disease, stroke, and diabetes.
- Unmanaged stress can lead to anxiety, depression, emotional exhaustion, and impaired cognitive function. The National Institute of Mental Health states that over 40 million adults in the U.S. have an anxiety disorder, and stress is often a trigger or exacerbating factor.
- A Gallup's global emotion report in 2019 states that about one-third of people around the world reported feeling stressed, worried, and/or angry. According to the 2020 report by the American Psychological Association, almost half of adults in the United States (49%) acknowledge that stress has had a detrimental impact on their behavior.

Burnout's Burning Effects

1. While related to stress, burnout specifically refers to chronic workplace stress leading to emotional, physical, and mental exhaustion. A 2020 Gallup study revealed that 52% of U.S. employees experience burnout, with millennials and Gen Z reporting even higher rates.
2. Burnout erodes motivation, engagement, and productivity. A 2017 study by the American Psychological Association estimated that workplace stress costs U.S. businesses roughly $500 billion annually due to absenteeism, presenteeism (reduced productivity while at work), and employee turnover.
3. Beyond work, burnout spills over into personal life, affecting relationships, hobbies, and overall well-being.

Beyond Numbers: Human Impact

Statistics paint a grim picture, but remember, they represent real people struggling with real burdens. Stress and burnout can:

Stifle potential: They can hinder creative thinking, problem-solving abilities, and overall performance, both professionally and personally.

Strain relationships: Irritability, emotional exhaustion, and decreased communication can negatively impact relationships with loved ones.

Reduce quality of life: The inability to enjoy activities or hobbies, coupled with physical and mental health issues, can significantly reduce overall well-being.

Chapter 1: Understanding Stress and Burnout

It is essential to understand these cankerworms in order to maintain mental and physical well-being in today's fast-paced world. While stress is a natural response to challenging situations, burnout is a more serious condition characterized by emotional exhaustion, cynicism, and reduced effectiveness in both personal and professional realms.

Stress

Stress is the body's natural response to demands or pressures perceived as threats. It triggers the release of hormones like cortisol and adrenaline, preparing the body to respond to perceived danger. Stress can result from various factors, including work pressures, relationship conflicts, financial worries, health problems, and major life changes.

Symptoms of stress can manifest physically (e.g., headaches, muscle tension), emotionally (e.g., irritability, anxiety), cognitively (e.g., difficulty concentrating), and behaviorally (e.g., changes in appetite or sleep patterns).

Effective stress management involves identifying stressors, developing coping strategies (such as relaxation techniques, time management, and seeking social support), and prioritizing self-care activities.

Importance of Stress Management

Stress management is crucial for maintaining overall well-being and preventing the negative effects of chronic stress on physical, mental, and emotional health. Here's why stress management is important:

Physical Health: Chronic stress can take a toll on the body, leading to a range of health problems such as high blood pressure, heart disease, weakened immune system, digestive issues, and chronic pain. By managing stress effectively, individuals can reduce their risk of developing these health conditions and promote better physical health.

Mental Health: Prolonged stress can also have significant effects on mental health, contributing to anxiety, depression, mood swings, and other mental health disorders. Stress management techniques such as relaxation exercises, mindfulness, and seeking support can help individuals cope with stressors and maintain optimal mental well-being.

Emotional Well-being: Unmanaged stress can exacerbate emotional challenges, leading to feelings of irritability, frustration, anger, and emotional exhaustion. Stress management strategies help individuals regulate their emotions, build resilience, and cultivate a positive outlook on life, fostering greater emotional well-being and stability.

Cognitive Functioning: Chronic stress can impair cognitive function, affecting memory, concentration, decision-making, and problem-solving abilities. By managing stress effectively, individuals can maintain optimal cognitive functioning and performance in various areas of life, including work, school, and personal relationships.

Quality of Life: Ultimately, stress management is essential for improving overall quality of life. By reducing stress levels and promoting a sense of balance, individuals can enjoy better relationships, increased productivity, enhanced creativity, and a greater sense of fulfillment and satisfaction in life.

Longevity: Research suggests that chronic stress may contribute to premature aging and reduced lifespan. By managing stress effectively and adopting healthy coping mechanisms, individuals can promote longevity and increase their chances of living a longer, healthier life.

Overall, stress management is essential for promoting physical health, mental well-being, emotional stability, cognitive functioning, and overall quality of life. By prioritizing stress management techniques and incorporating them into daily life, individuals can protect themselves against the harmful effects of stress and cultivate greater resilience and vitality.

Burnout

Burnout is a state of chronic stress characterized by emotional exhaustion, depersonalization (cynicism or detachment), and reduced personal accomplishment. Burnout often occurs as a result of prolonged exposure to stress, particularly in demanding work environments where individuals feel overwhelmed, unsupported, and lacking in control.

Here are the major symptoms of burnout. Burnout often begins with feelings of emotional exhaustion, where individuals feel drained, depleted, and overwhelmed by the demands of their work or other responsibilities. They may experience a sense of fatigue that persists despite adequate rest, leading to a loss of energy and enthusiasm.

As burnout progresses, individuals may develop a negative or cynical attitude toward their work, colleagues, or clients. They may become emotionally detached, distant, or indifferent, and may exhibit behaviors such as sarcasm, irritability, or avoidance of interpersonal interactions.

Burnout can also lead to a diminished sense of personal accomplishment or efficacy. Individuals may feel like they're no longer making a meaningful impact in their work or that their efforts are futile. They may experience feelings of inadequacy, self-doubt, or low self-esteem, despite past achievements or successes.

Causes of Burnout

High job demands, excessive workload, long hours, and tight deadlines can contribute to burnout. Lack of autonomy or control over one's work, unclear expectations, and role ambiguity can also increase feelings of stress and burnout.

Organizational culture, leadership styles, and workplace policies can influence burnout risk. Poor communication, lack of support from supervisors or coworkers, and limited opportunities for growth or advancement can contribute to feelings of disengagement and burnout.

Difficulty balancing work responsibilities with personal or family commitments can lead to burnout. When individuals feel like they have little time or energy for leisure activities, self-care, or relationships outside of work, they may experience increased stress and burnout.

Fear of job loss, layoffs, or restructuring can create a sense of uncertainty and anxiety, contributing to burnout. Employees who perceive their jobs as unstable or insecure may feel heightened stress and pressure to perform, leading to burnout over time.

When there's a disconnect between an individual's values, beliefs, and the culture or mission of their workplace, they may experience feelings of disillusionment or moral distress, contributing to burnout.

Individual characteristics such as perfectionism, high levels of self-criticism, or difficulty setting boundaries can also increase susceptibility to burnout. People who have a strong sense of duty or responsibility, and who struggle to say no or prioritize their own needs, may be at greater risk of burnout.

Overall, burnout is a complex phenomenon influenced by a combination of individual, organizational, and environmental factors.

Since we have seen that burnout comes from stress, it is good we learn more about stress and how to recognise it.

Chapter 2: Recognizing Stress

Identifying stress is the initial stage in effectively handling it. Here are several typical indications and manifestations of stress to be aware of:

Symptoms of Stress

1. Physical Symptoms: These include headaches, muscle tension or pain, fatigue or low energy, digestive problems, sleep disturbances (insomnia or oversleeping, rapid heartbeat or chest pain, sweating or trembling, changes in appetite (overeating or undereating), weakened immune system (frequent illnesses).

2. Psychological Indications: These encompass irritability or mood swings, anxiety or uneasiness, despondency or feelings of sorrow, sensation of being overwhelmed or losing control, incessant thoughts or constant fretting, restlessness or agitation, absence of

drive or enthusiasm, trouble unwinding or settling down.

3. Cognitive Symptoms: The cognitive symptoms are difficulty concentrating or focusing, forgetfulness or memory problems, racing thoughts or mind going blank, poor judgment or decision-making, negative self-talk or self-criticism, obsessive thinking or rumination.

4. Behavioral Symptoms: Here you will find changes in appetite or eating habits, Increased use of alcohol, drugs, or tobacco, withdrawal from social activities or hobbies, procrastination or avoidance of responsibilities, nail-biting, pacing, or other nervous habits, restlessness or fidgeting, difficulty completing tasks or making decisions, changes in sleep patterns or hygiene habits.

5. Interpersonal Symptoms: Here you'll see relationship conflicts or tension, social withdrawal or isolation, difficulty communicating effectively, irritability or impatience with others, reduced

empathy or compassion, and increased arguments or disagreements.

Recognizing these signs and symptoms of stress can help individuals take proactive steps to manage their stress levels effectively. It's important to pay attention to physical and emotional cues and changes in behavior and interpersonal relationships.

Identifying Sources of Stress

Identifying sources of stress is essential for developing effective stress management strategies. Here are some common sources of stress to consider:

Work-related Stressors
- High workloads or tight deadlines
- Job insecurity or fear of layoffs
- Conflict with coworkers or supervisors
- Lack of control over work tasks or schedule
- Long hours or overtime
- Commuting or transportation issues
- Work-life imbalance

Financial Stressors
- Debt or financial insecurity
- Unemployment or loss of income
- Unexpected expenses or emergencies
- Living beyond one's means
- Retirement planning or savings concerns
- Inflation or economic instability

Relationship Stressors

* ❖ Marital conflicts or relationship problems
* ❖ Divorce or separation
* ❖ Parenting challenges
* ❖ Caregiving responsibilities
* ❖ Social isolation or loneliness
* ❖ Conflicts with family members or friends

Health-related Stressors

- ☐ Chronic illness or health conditions
- ☐ Injury or disability
- ☐ Pain or discomfort
- ☐ Medical treatments or procedures
- ☐ Concerns about aging or mortality
- ☐ Unhealthy lifestyle habits (e.g., poor diet, lack of exercise)

Life Events

- → Moving or relocation
- → Marriage or starting a family
- → Bereavement or loss of a loved one
- → Graduation or career changes
- → Major life transitions (e.g., retirement)
- → Legal issues or disputes

Environmental Stressors

- ➢ Pollution or environmental hazards
- ➢ Noise pollution
- ➢ Crowded or chaotic living conditions
- ➢ Natural disasters or emergencies

➢ Climate change or extreme weather events

Personal Stressors
- Perfectionism or unrealistic expectations
- Self-doubt or low self-esteem
- Lack of assertiveness or boundaries
- Negative thinking patterns
- Past traumas or unresolved issues
- Lack of leisure or relaxation time

By identifying the specific sources of stress in your life, you can develop targeted strategies to address and manage them effectively. This may involve making lifestyle changes, setting boundaries, seeking support, or practicing stress-reduction techniques such as relaxation, mindfulness, or exercise.

Differences Between Stress and Burnout

Stress and burnout are related but distinct concepts, each with its own set of characteristics and consequences. Here are the key differences between stress and burnout.

Attribute	Stress	Burnout
Nature	A natural and adaptive response to perceived threats or demands.	A more severe and chronic condition, often resulting from prolonged exposure to stressors.
Duration	Typically short-term and temporary.	A long-term and persistent condition that can develop gradually over time.
Causes	Can result from various sources, including work pressures, relationship conflicts, finances, health, and major life changes.	Often the result of prolonged exposure to chronic stress, particularly in demanding work environments.
Symptoms	Can include physical, emotional, cognitive, and behavioral symptoms.	Emotional exhaustion, depersonalization, and diminished personal achievement are the defining features.
Impact	Negative effects on physical and mental health if	Significant consequences for individuals'

	left unmanaged, typically do not lead to the profound sense of disengagement and disillusionment associated with burnout.	well-being, including increased risk of depression, anxiety, substance abuse, cardiovascular disease, and impaired job performance.
Treatment and Prevention	Stress management techniques like relaxation, time management, and seeking social support can help.	May require more intensive interventions, like taking time off work, seeking therapy or counseling, reassessing work-life balance, and making changes to reduce job-related stressors.

Overall, while stress and burnout share some similarities, burnout is a more severe and chronic condition that can have significant long-term consequences if left unaddressed. Recognizing the differences between stress and burnout is essential for identifying appropriate interventions.

The Impact of Stress and Burnout
The impact of stress and burnout can be profound, affecting individuals' physical, mental, emotional, and social well-being in various ways:

Physical Health: Prolonged stress can contribute to a range of physical health problems, including high blood pressure, heart disease, weakened immune system, digestive issues, headaches, muscle tension, and chronic pain. Burnout is associated with an increased risk of physical health conditions such as cardiovascular disease, gastrointestinal disorders, immune system dysfunction, and chronic fatigue syndrome.

Mental Health: Chronic stress can have significant effects on mental health, increasing the risk of anxiety disorders, depression, mood swings, panic attacks, and other mental health issues. Burnout is closely linked to mental health problems, including depression, anxiety, emotional instability, and feelings of hopelessness or despair.

Emotional Well-being: Stress can lead to emotional challenges such as irritability, frustration, anger, mood swings, and emotional exhaustion. Individuals may experience difficulty regulating their emotions and may feel overwhelmed or out of control. While:

Burnout is characterized by emotional exhaustion, depersonalization (cynicism or detachment), and reduced personal accomplishment. Individuals may feel emotionally drained, detached from their work or relationships, and may experience feelings of cynicism, apathy, or emptiness.

Cognitive Functioning: Chronic stress can impair cognitive function, affecting memory, concentration, decision-making, and problem-solving abilities. Individuals may experience difficulty focusing, remembering information, and making sound judgments.

Burnout can lead to cognitive deficits such as decreased attention, reduced creativity, impaired decision-making, and poor problem-solving skills. Individuals may struggle to maintain focus, stay organized, and perform effectively in their roles.

Work Performance: High levels of stress can negatively impact work performance, leading to decreased productivity, increased absenteeism, higher error rates, and reduced job satisfaction. While burnout is associated with diminished job performance, including decreased motivation, lower productivity, increased likelihood of making mistakes, and reduced engagement with work tasks.

Interpersonal Relationships: Chronic stress can strain interpersonal relationships, leading to conflicts, communication breakdowns, and decreased intimacy or connection with others. Burnout can affect relationships both at work and in personal life, as individuals may become emotionally detached, withdrawn, or irritable. They may have difficulty connecting with others, expressing empathy, or maintaining healthy boundaries.

Overall, the impact of stress and burnout extends beyond individual well-being to affect job performance, relationships, and overall quality of life. Recognizing the signs and symptoms of stress and burnout and taking proactive steps to manage them effectively are essential for promoting resilience, preventing long-term health problems, and fostering greater well-being.

Assessing Your Stress and Burnout Levels

Assessing your stress and burnout levels is an important first step in addressing these issues and implementing effective coping strategies. Here are some self-assessment tools and techniques to help you evaluate your stress and burnout levels:

Stress Assessment Tools

Stress Questionnaires: Use validated stress questionnaires or surveys to assess your current stress levels. These tools typically ask about your experiences with stressors, symptoms of stress, and how stress is impacting various areas of your life.

Stress Diary: Keep a stress diary to track your stressors, triggers, and symptoms over time. Note the situations, events, or thoughts that cause you to stress, as well as your physical, emotional, and behavioral responses.

Stress Rating Scale: Rate your stress levels on a scale from 1 to 10 at different times throughout the day or week. Pay attention to patterns and trends in your stress levels to identify when you're feeling most stressed and what factors contribute to it.

Burnout Assessment Tools

Maslach Burnout Inventory (MBI): The MBI is a widely used assessment tool designed to measure burnout across three dimensions: emotional exhaustion, depersonalization, and reduced personal accomplishment. It consists of a series of questions that evaluate your experiences and feelings related to burnout.

Copenhagen Burnout Inventory (CBI): The CBI assesses burnout across three domains: personal burnout, work-related burnout, and client-related burnout. It includes questions about your experiences with physical and psychological exhaustion, as well as feelings of cynicism and incompetence.

Burnout Self-Test: Take a self-test or questionnaire specifically designed to assess burnout symptoms and risk factors. These tests typically ask about your experiences with emotional exhaustion, detachment, and reduced effectiveness in various areas of your life.

Reflective Techniques

Journaling: Spend some time journaling about your experiences with stress and burnout. Write about your thoughts, feelings, and reactions to stressors, as well as any changes you've noticed in your mood, behavior, or physical health.

Self-Reflection: Take some time for self-reflection to evaluate your current stress and burnout levels. Consider how you're feeling physically, emotionally, mentally, and socially, and whether you're experiencing any signs or symptoms of stress or burnout.

Talk to Others: Seek feedback from friends, family members, or colleagues about your behavior, mood, and overall well-being. Sometimes others can provide valuable insights into how you're coping with stress and whether they've noticed any changes in your behavior or attitude.

By using these assessment tools and techniques, you can gain a better understanding of your stress and burnout levels, identify areas of concern, and take proactive steps to manage your well-being effectively. If you find that your stress or burnout levels are high, consider seeking support from a healthcare professional or mental health provider for further evaluation and guidance.

Self-Assessment Tools and Questionnaires

Self-assessment tools and questionnaires are valuable resources for individuals to evaluate their stress and burnout levels. Here are some commonly used self-assessment tools and questionnaires for stress and burnout:

Perceived Stress Scale (PSS): This is a commonly utilized questionnaire that helps individuals assess the level of stress they perceive in various situations in their lives. It consists of several statements about feelings and thoughts over the past month, with respondents rating how often they experience each item on a scale from 0 to 4.

Holmes and Rahe Stress Scale: The Holmes and Rahe Stress Scale is a tool that measures the impact of major life events on stress levels. It assigns a numerical value to various life events (e.g., marriage, job change, illness) based on the level of stress they are likely to induce. Individuals tally up their scores to determine their overall stress level.

Maslach Burnout Inventory (MBI): The Maslach Burnout Inventory is a widely used assessment tool for measuring burnout. It consists of three subscales: emotional exhaustion, depersonalization, and reduced personal accomplishment. Respondents rate how frequently they experience various feelings and behaviors related to burnout on a scale from 0 to 6.

Copenhagen Burnout Inventory (CBI): The Copenhagen Burnout Inventory assesses burnout across three domains: personal burnout, work-related burnout, and client-related burnout. It includes questions about physical and psychological exhaustion, as well as feelings of cynicism and incompetence.

Stress Diary: A stress diary is a self-assessment tool that allows individuals to track their stressors, triggers, and symptoms over time. It involves recording details about stressful situations, thoughts, emotions, physical sensations, and coping strategies on a daily or weekly basis. You get a free with the purchase of the paperback and hardcover of this book.

Self-Reflection Worksheets: Self-reflection worksheets provide prompts and questions for individuals to reflect on their experiences with stress and burnout, as well as their coping strategies, strengths, and areas for improvement. These worksheets can help individuals gain insight into their stressors, reactions, and needs.

Online Self-Assessment Tools: There are many online resources and websites that offer free self-assessment tools and quizzes for stress and burnout. These tools typically provide instant feedback and personalized recommendations based on individuals' responses.

Using these self-assessment tools and questionnaires, individuals can gain insight into their stress and burnout levels, identify areas of concern, and develop targeted strategies for coping and self-care. It's important to remember that self-assessment tools are just one part of the process, and seeking support from healthcare professionals or mental health providers may be beneficial for further evaluation and guidance.

Chapter 3: Combating the Stress Monster

The good news is, we're not powerless. There are coping strategies we can use for stress management. These are essential for maintaining well-being and resilience in the face of life's challenges.

Some of the ways to manage stress and prevent burnout are by using techniques such as mindfulness meditation, relaxation exercises, and deep breathing can help regulate the nervous system and reduce stress levels. Also maintaining a healthy lifestyle and prioritizing time management helps.

It is important to remember that prioritizing your well-being is not a luxury, but rather a necessity. Now let's discuss these techniques in more detail.

Relaxation Techniques

Relaxation techniques are valuable tools for managing stress, promoting relaxation, and improving overall well-being. Here are some commonly used relaxation techniques:

Deep Breathing: One effective way to promote relaxation and reduce stress is through the practice of deep breathing exercises. The main action is to inhale deeply through your nose, hold your breath for a few seconds, and exhale slowly through your mouth. Here are the steps to use deep breathing.

- To begin, find a comfortable position, whether it be sitting or lying down.
- Close your eyes and take a slow, deep breath in through your nose, filling your lungs with air.
- Hold your breath for a few seconds, then exhale slowly and completely through your mouth, letting go of tension and stress.

- Perform this rhythmic breathing sequence multiple times, concentrating on the feeling of air flowing in and out of your body.

Progressive Muscle Relaxation (PMR): Tense and then relax each muscle group in your body, starting from your toes and working your way up to your head, to release physical tension and promote relaxation. Here are the steps:
- Begin the relaxation process by tensing the muscles in one part of your body, such as your hands or shoulders, for a few seconds before releasing the tension.
- Then, release the tension and allow the muscles to relax completely, noticing the difference between tension and relaxation.
- Continue this process, gradually moving through each muscle group in your body, from your feet to your head.
- Focus on the sensations of warmth and heaviness as your muscles relax, letting go of any stress or tension you may be holding onto.

Mindfulness Meditation: Engage in mindfulness meditation to develop awareness of the present moment and alleviate stress. Focus on your breath, sensations in your body, or sounds in your environment without judgment.

- Locate a serene and undisturbed environment.
- Gently shut your eyes and focus your attention on your breath, observing the sensations of each inhalation and exhalation.
- As thoughts or distractions arise, gently acknowledge them without judgment, and then return your focus to your breath.
- Allow yourself to be fully present in the moment, observing your thoughts, emotions, and sensations as they come and go.
- Practice mindfulness meditation for a few minutes or longer, depending on your preference and availability.

Guided Imagery: This is another relaxation technique you can use to relieve stress and prevent burnout. Here are the steps:

- Close your eyes and visualize a peaceful, calming scene, such as a beach, forest, or mountaintop.
- Imagine yourself fully immersed in this scene, noticing the sights, sounds, smells, and sensations around you.
- Engage your senses and explore the details of the imagery, allowing yourself to relax and let go of any tension or stress.
- You can use guided imagery recordings or scripts to guide you through the visualization process or create your own imagery based on your preferences.

Breath Counting: Counting your breath is another relaxation technique that can help with stress and burnout. Here are the steps:

- Assume a relaxed posture, either sitting or lying down, and close your eyes.
- Take a deep breath in through your nose, counting silently to yourself as you inhale.
- Then, exhale slowly and completely through your mouth, counting again as you breathe out.
- Continue this pattern, counting each inhale and exhale, focusing your

attention on the rhythm of your breath and the counting process.
- If you lose count or become distracted, simply start over again from one, without judgment or frustration.

These relaxation techniques can be practiced individually or combined to create a personalized relaxation routine that suits your preferences and needs. Regular practice of these techniques can help reduce stress, promote relaxation, and improve overall well-being.

Time Management and Prioritization

Time management and prioritization are essential skills for effectively managing workload, reducing stress, and achieving goals. Here are some strategies for improving time management and prioritization:

Create a Schedule: Organize your time by creating a daily or weekly schedule that includes time for work, leisure, self-care, and relaxation. Allocate specific blocks of time for different activities, including work, personal tasks, leisure activities, and self-care. Establish a daily or weekly routine that includes dedicated time for focused work, breaks, and relaxation.

Establish Priorities: Determine the tasks that hold the utmost significance and arrange them in order of urgency and importance. Break large tasks into smaller, manageable steps to avoid feeling overwhelmed. Use prioritization techniques such as the Eisenhower Matrix (urgent vs. important) or the ABCDE method (assigning priority labels) to categorize tasks and determine which ones to tackle first. Focus on completing high-priority tasks that align with your goals and values, while delegating or deferring lower-priority tasks when possible.

Use Time Management Tools: Utilize tools such as calendars, planners, task lists, or digital apps to organize your schedule and keep track of deadlines and commitments. Allocate specific blocks of time for different activities, such as work, exercise, and socializing, to maintain balance and structure in your day. Break down large tasks into smaller, manageable steps to make them more achievable and less overwhelming.

Set Clear Goals and Priorities: Identify your short-term and long-term goals, both personally and professionally. Prioritize your goals based on their importance and urgency, focusing on tasks that will have the greatest impact. Clarify your goals, values, and priorities to guide your decision-making. Concentrate on what holds the greatest value to you and distribute your time and energy accordingly. Break larger goals or projects into smaller, more manageable tasks or milestones. Set specific, achievable objectives for each step and celebrate your progress along the way.

Avoid Multitasking: Focus on one task at a time, giving it your full attention and concentration to maximize efficiency and effectiveness. Multitasking can lead to decreased productivity, increased errors, and higher levels of stress. Learn to set boundaries around your time and commitments, saying no to requests or activities that don't align with your priorities or goals. Be assertive in communicating your limits and managing expectations with others, both at work and in your personal life.

Limit Screen Time: Set boundaries around your use of technology and social media to prevent information overload and reduce stress. Schedule regular breaks from screens to recharge and relax. Designate specific times for work-related tasks and prioritize time for leisure, relaxation, and activities that bring you joy.

Manage Procrastination: Identify the underlying reasons for procrastination, such as fear of failure, perfectionism, or lack of motivation. Break tasks into smaller, more manageable steps, and use techniques such as the Pomodoro Technique (working in focused intervals) to overcome procrastination and maintain momentum.

Setting Boundaries and Saying No

Setting boundaries and learning to say no are essential skills for maintaining balance, protecting your time and energy, and fostering healthy relationships. Here are some strategies for setting boundaries and asserting yourself effectively:

Know Your Limits: Reflect on your values, priorities, and needs to determine what is most important to you. Identify your physical, emotional, and mental limits, as well as the activities or situations that drain your energy or cause you stress. Recognize that it's okay to say no to requests, invitations, or obligations that don't align with your priorities or values.

Clarify Your Boundaries: Clearly define your boundaries by identifying what behaviors, requests, or interactions are acceptable and unacceptable to you. Communicate your boundaries assertively and respectfully to others, using "I" statements to express your needs and preferences. Offer a brief explanation if necessary, but avoid over-explaining or making excuses for your choices.

Practice Assertiveness: Assertiveness involves expressing your thoughts, feelings, and preferences in a direct, honest, and respectful manner. Use assertive communication techniques, such as maintaining eye contact, speaking calmly and confidently, and using assertive body language (e.g., standing tall, maintaining open posture). Be firm and decisive in your response, without feeling the need to justify or apologize for your decision.

Practice phrases such as
"I'm not comfortable with that,"
"I need some time to myself," or
"I have other commitments right now."

Be Consistent: Consistently enforce your boundaries and say no when necessary, even if it feels uncomfortable or difficult at first. Avoid giving in to guilt, pressure, or manipulation from others, and prioritize your own well-being and needs. Use assertive language to communicate your boundaries and preferences clearly and directly.

Practice Self-Care: Prioritize self-care and self-compassion to maintain your physical, emotional, and mental well-being. Take time to recharge, rest, and engage in activities that bring you joy and fulfillment.

Setting boundaries and saying no are skills that require practice and reinforcement over time. You can cultivate healthier relationships, reduce stress, and enhance your overall quality of life by prioritizing your own needs and respecting your boundaries.

Healthy Lifestyle Habits

Healthy lifestyle habits are essential for maintaining physical, mental, and emotional well-being. Outlined below are several fundamental elements of a well-balanced lifestyle:

Regular Exercise: Engage in regular physical activity, such as walking, jogging, yoga, or dancing, to reduce stress hormones and promote relaxation. Aim for at least 30 minutes of moderate exercise most days of the week. Engage in regular physical activity to improve cardiovascular health, boost mood, reduce stress, and enhance overall well-being. Aim for at least 150 minutes of moderate-intensity exercise or 75 minutes of vigorous-intensity exercise per week, along with muscle-strengthening activities on two or more days per week. Choose activities you enjoy, such as walking, running, cycling, swimming, dancing, or playing sports, and vary your routine to keep it interesting and challenging.

Healthy Eating: Maintain a balanced diet rich in fruits, vegetables, whole grains, lean proteins, and healthy fats to support overall health and well-being. Avoid excessive caffeine, sugar, and processed foods, which can contribute to stress. Maintain a balanced diet rich in fruits, vegetables, whole grains, lean proteins, and healthy fats to provide essential nutrients and fuel your body. Limit consumption of processed foods, sugary snacks, and high-fat, high-calorie foods that contribute to weight gain and increase the risk of chronic diseases.
Practice mindful eating by paying attention to hunger and fullness cues, savoring your food, and eating slowly to prevent overeating.

Adequate Sleep: Prioritize good sleep hygiene by establishing a regular sleep schedule, creating a relaxing bedtime routine, and creating a sleep-friendly environment. It is crucial to strive for 7-9 hours of restful sleep every night in order to ensure optimal health and prevent exhaustion. Prioritize good sleep hygiene by establishing a regular sleep schedule and bedtime routine that allows for 7-9 hours of quality sleep per night. Create a sleep-friendly environment by minimizing noise, light, and electronic distractions in the bedroom, and ensuring your mattress and pillows are comfortable and supportive. Avoid caffeine, alcohol, and heavy meals close to bedtime, and engage in relaxing activities such as reading or taking a warm bath to promote relaxation and prepare for sleep.

Hydration: Drink plenty of water throughout the day to stay hydrated and support bodily functions such as digestion, circulation, and temperature regulation. Aim for at least 8-10 cups of water per day, or more if you're physically active or in hot weather, and listen to your body's thirst signals to ensure adequate hydration.

Limiting Alcohol and Tobacco: Limit alcohol consumption to moderate levels (up to one drink per day for women and up to two drinks per day for men) to reduce the risk of health problems such as liver disease, heart disease, and certain types of cancer. Avoid smoking and exposure to secondhand smoke, as smoking is a leading cause of preventable death and is associated with numerous health risks, including lung cancer, heart disease, and respiratory problems.

Seeking Social Support: Reach out to friends, family members, or support groups for emotional support and encouragement. Talking to others can help you feel heard, understood, and less alone in your struggles. Don't be afraid to express your feelings and emotions to trusted individuals. Sharing your concerns and experiences can help alleviate stress and foster deeper connections.

Yoga and Tai Chi: Practice yoga or tai chi to promote relaxation, reduce muscle tension, and improve flexibility and balance. These mind-body practices combine physical movement with breath awareness and meditation.

Journaling: Write in a journal regularly to express your thoughts, feelings, and concerns. Journaling can help you gain clarity, process emotions, and identify patterns or triggers for stress. You can use the attached stress diary as a journal for this.

Review and Adjust: Regularly review your schedule and task list to assess progress, identify obstacles, and make adjustments as needed. Be flexible and adaptable in responding to changes in priorities, deadlines, or circumstances, adjusting your schedule and plans accordingly.

Incorporating these healthy lifestyle habits into your daily routine can have a positive impact on your physical health, mental well-being, and overall quality of life. Start with small, achievable changes and gradually build upon them over time to create a sustainable and balanced lifestyle that supports your health and happiness.

Chapter 4: Preventing and Managing Burnout (9 Ways)

Preventing and managing burnout is crucial for maintaining well-being and productivity, especially in demanding work environments. Here are some strategies to help prevent and manage burnout:

1. Recognize the Signs of Burnout

Be aware of the signs and symptoms of burnout, such as chronic fatigue, cynicism, decreased productivity, irritability, and physical symptoms like headaches or gastrointestinal issues. Monitor your physical, emotional, and mental well-being regularly to detect early warning signs of burnout and take proactive steps to address them.

2. Set Realistic Expectations

Setting realistic expectations is crucial for preventing burnout and maintaining well-being. Establish realistic expectations for yourself in terms of workload, deadlines, and performance standards. Avoid overcommitting or taking on more responsibilities than you can handle, and be willing to renegotiate or delegate tasks when necessary. Set realistic expectations for yourself in terms of workload, deadlines, and performance standards. Avoid overcommitting or taking on more responsibilities than you can handle, and be willing to say no when necessary.

3. Communicate Effectively

Communicate openly and honestly with your employer, colleagues, and loved ones about your needs and priorities. Advocate for yourself and assertively communicate your boundaries and limitations to ensure they are respected. Communicate your expectations, boundaries, and limitations clearly and assertively with others. Be transparent about what you can realistically deliver and negotiate agreements that are mutually acceptable.

4. Prioritize Self-Care

Make self-care a priority by incorporating activities that promote relaxation, stress reduction, and well-being into your daily routine. Schedule regular breaks, engage in hobbies or leisure activities you enjoy, and prioritize sleep, exercise, and healthy eating habits. Find meaning and purpose in your work by aligning your values, interests, and strengths with your job responsibilities. Identify aspects of your work that are personally fulfilling or meaningful and focus on cultivating those areas to increase satisfaction and engagement.

5. Establish Work-Life Balance

Achieving a healthy equilibrium between work and personal life is vital for overall well-being and avoiding burnout. Set boundaries between work and personal life to prevent work from encroaching on your time, energy, and relationships. Create designated times for work, relaxation, and socializing, and strive to maintain a healthy balance between professional and personal commitments.

6. Practice Stress Management Techniques

Incorporate stress management techniques such as deep breathing, meditation, yoga, or mindfulness into your daily routine to reduce stress and promote relaxation. Identify sources of stress in your life and develop coping strategies to manage them effectively, such as time management, problem-solving, or seeking social support.

7. Take Breaks and Vacations

Take regular breaks throughout the day to rest, recharge, and prevent burnout. Schedule time off for vacations or personal days to relax, rejuvenate, and disconnect from work-related stressors. Take regular breaks from technology and disconnect from work-related emails, calls, and messages outside of work hours. Create designated times for digital detoxing to promote relaxation, recharge, and focus on non-work activities.

8. Seek Professional Help if Needed

If you're experiencing persistent symptoms of burnout or are struggling to cope, seek professional help from a counselor, therapist, or mental health provider. Therapy or counseling can provide support, guidance, and coping strategies to help you manage burnout effectively and regain a sense of balance and well-being. Seek feedback from trusted individuals, such as colleagues, mentors, or friends, to gain perspective on your expectations and goals. Don't hesitate to ask for help or support when needed, and be open to receiving assistance from others.

9. Celebrate Progress, Not Perfection
Emphasize growth rather than flawlessness and commemorate your accomplishments, regardless of their magnitude. Acknowledge your efforts and accomplishments, and give yourself credit for the steps you've taken towards your goals. Acknowledge that unexpected challenges or obstacles may arise, and be prepared to adjust your expectations and plans accordingly. Embrace a flexible mindset and view setbacks as opportunities for learning and growth.

Building a Support System

Seeking support and building a strong support system is essential for maintaining mental, emotional, and social well-being. Here are some strategies for seeking support and nurturing meaningful connections with others:

- ***Identify Trusted Individuals:*** Identify individuals in your life whom you trust and feel comfortable confiding in. This may include friends, family members, colleagues, mentors, or mental health professionals.

- ***Communicate Your Needs***: Be open and honest about your feelings, experiences, and needs with those you trust. Clearly communicate what type of support you're seeking and how others can best help you.

- ***Reach Out for Help:*** Don't hesitate to reach out for help when you're struggling or in need of support. Reach out to friends or loved ones for emotional support, encouragement, or advice.

- ***Participate in Social Activities:*** Engage in social activities and spend time with friends, family, or community groups. Participate in activities that bring you joy, relaxation, and connection with others.

- ***Join Support Groups:*** Consider joining a support group or community organization where you can connect with others who share similar experiences or challenges. Support groups offer a secure environment for exchanging experiences, receiving support, and acquiring coping techniques.

- ***Offer Support to Others:*** Offer support and kindness to others in your life who may be going through difficult times. Show empathy, listen actively, and offer practical assistance or emotional support when needed. Practice active listening when supporting others, giving them your full attention and empathy. Validate their feelings and experiences, and avoid judgment or criticism.

- ***Cultivate Healthy Relationships:*** Nurture healthy, supportive relationships with friends, family members, and colleagues. Surround yourself with people who uplift and encourage you, and minimize interactions with individuals who drain your energy or undermine your well-being.

- ***Seek support:*** Seek support from your employer, colleagues, or support networks if you're feeling overwhelmed or struggling to maintain a work-life balance. Reach out for help when needed, and don't hesitate to ask for accommodations or support to help you better manage your responsibilities.

- ***Seek Professional Help:*** If you're struggling with mental health issues or need additional support, don't hesitate to seek professional help. A therapist, counselor, or mental health professional can provide personalized support, guidance, and treatment to help you navigate challenges and build resilience.

By building a support system, you can enhance your resilience, cope more effectively with stress, and foster greater well-being and fulfillment in your life. Remember that asking for help is a sign of strength, not weakness and that you don't have to face challenges alone.

Recognizing and Addressing Negative Thought Patterns

Recognizing and addressing negative thought patterns is an important aspect of maintaining mental well-being and promoting positive thinking. Here are some strategies for recognizing and addressing negative thought patterns:

Increase self-awareness by practicing mindfulness techniques, such as meditation or mindful breathing. Observe your thoughts without judgment and notice when negative thoughts arise. Counter pessimistic thoughts by scrutinizing their truthfulness and legitimacy. Ask yourself if there is evidence to support the negative thought and consider alternative, more balanced perspectives.

Practice cognitive restructuring techniques to reframe negative thoughts into more positive or neutral ones. Identify cognitive distortions, such as black-and-white thinking or catastrophizing, and replace them with more realistic and balanced thoughts. Practice self-compassion by treating yourself with kindness and understanding, especially when experiencing negative thoughts or emotions. Offer yourself the same level of empathy and support that you would offer to a friend in a similar situation.

Nurture a feeling of thankfulness by concentrating on the favorable aspects of your life and expressing gratitude for your possessions. Keep a gratitude journal and write down three things you're grateful for each day to shift your focus away from negativity. Limit exposure to negative influences, such as negative news, social media comparisons, or toxic relationships. Surround yourself with positive, supportive people and environments that uplift and inspire you.

Use positive affirmations to counteract negative self-talk and build self-esteem and confidence. Repeat affirmations such as "*I am capable,*" "*I am worthy,*" "*I am deserving of happiness*" or "*I am enough*" to challenge negative beliefs and reinforce positive ones.

If negative thought patterns persist and interfere with your daily life or well-being, consider seeking professional help from a therapist or counselor. A mental health professional can provide support, guidance, and evidence-based techniques to help you address and manage negative thought patterns effectively.

Give priority to self-care activities that foster relaxation, diminish stress, and enhance your overall state of being. Engage in activities you enjoy, such as hobbies, exercise, or spending time in nature, to boost mood and counteract negativity. Practice acceptance of negative thoughts and emotions as natural and temporary aspects of the human experience. Practice letting go of attachment to negative thoughts and allow them to pass without getting caught up in them or dwelling on them.

By implementing these strategies, you can become more aware of negative thought patterns, challenge them effectively, and cultivate a more positive and resilient mindset over time. Remember that changing thought patterns takes practice and patience, so be gentle with yourself as you work towards greater mental well-being.

Creating a Resilient Mindset

Creating a resilient mindset is essential for navigating life's challenges, bouncing back from adversity, and thriving in the face of adversity. Here are some strategies for fostering resilience:

Cultivate self-awareness by reflecting on your thoughts, feelings, and reactions to stressors. Recognize your strengths, weaknesses, and areas for growth, and be honest with yourself about your limitations. Believe in your ability to develop new skills, overcome obstacles, and adapt to change over time.

Practice optimism by focusing on the positive aspects of situations and believing in your ability to overcome setbacks. Reframe negative experiences into learning opportunities and look for silver linings in difficult circumstances. Develop effective coping strategies for managing stress and adversity, such as problem-solving, emotion regulation, and seeking social support. Experiment with different coping techniques to find what works best for you and incorporate them into your daily routine.

Maintain perspective by stepping back from stressful situations and considering the bigger picture. Recognize that challenges are temporary and that you have overcome difficulties in the past, which can provide strength and resilience for the future. Cultivate strong social connections with friends, family members, colleagues, and community networks. Lean on your support system for encouragement, advice, and emotional support during challenging times.

Set realistic, achievable goals that align with your values, interests, and abilities. Break larger goals into smaller, manageable steps and celebrate your progress along the way. Prioritize your physical health by engaging in regular exercise, eating a balanced diet, getting enough sleep, and practicing relaxation techniques. Physical well-being is closely linked to mental resilience and can help you better cope with stressors. Find meaning and purpose in your life by pursuing activities and goals that align with your values and passions.

Connect with something larger than yourself, whether it's a cause, a belief system, or a sense of spirituality, to provide meaning and motivation during difficult times. Cultivating positive thinking is a powerful way to improve your outlook on life, enhance resilience, and increase overall well-being. Cultivate gratitude by focusing on the things you're thankful for in your life, big and small. Keep a gratitude journal and write down three things you're grateful for each day to train your brain to notice the positive aspects of your life.

Challenge negative thoughts and replace them with more balanced, realistic perspectives. Surround yourself with positive influences, such as supportive friends, uplifting music, inspiring books, or motivational quotes. Limit exposure to negative news, social media, or toxic environments that drain your energy and contribute to negative thinking. Repeat affirmations such as to reinforce positive beliefs about yourself.

Approach challenges with a problem-solving mindset and look for opportunities for growth and learning in difficult situations. Use visualization techniques to imagine yourself achieving your goals and living your best life. Picture yourself overcoming obstacles, reaching milestones, and experiencing feelings of joy, fulfillment, and success. Practice mindfulness to increase awareness of the present moment and cultivate a non-judgmental attitude towards your thoughts and experiences.

Notice when negative thoughts arise and gently redirect your attention to the present moment or positive aspects of your surroundings. Celebrate your successes and accomplishments, no matter how small. Acknowledge your progress and give yourself credit for the steps you've taken towards your goals. Seek out friendships and relationships that bring out the best in you and inspire you to be your authentic self.

By incorporating these strategies into your life, you can cultivate a resilient mindset that enables you to navigate challenges with courage, adaptability, and strength. Resilience is a skill that can be developed and strengthened over time, so be patient and compassionate with yourself as you work towards building greater resilience in your life.

Developing Coping Skills and Resilience
Developing coping skills and resilience is essential for navigating life's challenges, managing stress, and bouncing back from adversity. Here are some ways to do it.

Take time to identify the specific stressors or triggers in your life that contribute to feelings of stress or overwhelm. Recognize both external stressors (e.g., work deadlines, relationship conflicts) and internal stressors (e.g., negative self-talk, perfectionism). Practice stress management techniques such as deep breathing, progressive muscle relaxation, mindfulness meditation, or guided imagery. Experiment with different techniques to find what works best for you and incorporate them into your daily routine.

Build problem-solving skills to effectively address challenges and find solutions to difficult situations. Cultivate strong social connections and seek support from friends, family members, or support groups during times of stress or adversity. Share your feelings, concerns, and experiences with trusted individuals who can offer empathy, encouragement, and practical assistance. Develop emotional resilience by acknowledging and accepting your emotions, both positive and negative.

Cultivate a positive outlook by challenging negative thoughts and reframing them into more positive or balanced perspectives. Focus on gratitude, optimism, and solutions rather than dwelling on problems or setbacks. Break larger goals into smaller, manageable steps and celebrate your progress along the way.

Embrace flexibility and adaptability in the face of change or uncertainty.

Recognize that life is unpredictable, and develop the resilience to adjust your plans or expectations as needed. If you're struggling to cope with stress or experiencing persistent feelings of distress, don't hesitate to seek professional help from a therapist, counselor, or mental health provider. Therapy can provide support, guidance, and evidence-based techniques to help you develop coping skills and build resilience effectively.

By implementing these strategies and practicing resilience-building techniques, you can develop the coping skills needed to navigate life's challenges with strength, adaptability, and perseverance. Remember that resilience is a skill that can be learned and strengthened over time, and that seeking support is a sign of strength, not weakness.

Practicing gratitude and mindfulness arc powerful tools for promoting mental well-being, reducing stress, and increasing overall happiness. Express gratitude to others by writing thank-you notes, sending appreciation messages, or verbally expressing your appreciation. Take time to reflect on past experiences and identify lessons learned or silver linings in challenging situations. Make gratitude a daily habit by incorporating it into your morning or bedtime routine, or setting reminders throughout the day to pause and appreciate the good things in your life.

Practice mindfulness meditation by setting aside a few minutes each day to focus on your breath, bodily sensations, or the present moment. Engage in everyday activities mindfully by paying attention to your senses and fully immersing yourself in the experience. Practice mindful eating by savoring each bite, noticing the flavors, textures, and smells of your food, and eating without distractions.

Use mindfulness techniques to manage stress and anxiety, such as deep breathing, body scans, or progressive muscle relaxation. Cultivate a non-judgmental attitude towards your thoughts and emotions, allowing them to come and go without attachment or resistance.

Combine gratitude and mindfulness practices by expressing gratitude for the present moment and cultivating appreciation for the simple joys in life. Practice gratitude meditation by focusing

on feelings of gratitude and appreciation during
your mindfulness practice.

Chapter 5: Seeking Professional Help

Taking the initiative to seek professional assistance is a brave and significant stride towards enhancing your mental health and overall well-being. The first thing to do is to acknowledge when you're struggling with your mental health and recognize that seeking help is a sign of strength, not weakness. Be honest with yourself about the severity and impact of your symptoms on your daily life and functioning.

Educate yourself about different types of mental health professionals and treatment approaches, such as therapy, counseling, medication, or support groups. Consider your preferences, needs, and goals when exploring treatment options and choosing a provider.

Then look for a qualified and licensed mental health professional who has experience and expertise in treating your specific concerns or conditions. Seek recommendations from trusted sources, such as friends, family members, healthcare providers, or online directories.

Reach out to the mental health professional or provider you've chosen to schedule an initial appointment. Be prepared to discuss your concerns, symptoms, and goals for treatment during the first session.

The next thing is to be open and honest with your mental health provider about your thoughts, feelings, and experiences, even if they're difficult to talk about. Share relevant information about your medical history, current medications, and any past or ongoing treatments.

Collaborate with your mental health provider to develop a personalized treatment plan tailored to your needs and goals. Discuss different treatment options, interventions, and strategies to address your concerns and work towards recovery.

Commit to attending regular therapy or counseling sessions as recommended by your provider. Be consistent and engaged in the therapeutic process, actively participating in sessions and completing any assigned homework or exercises.

Follow through with any recommendations or referrals provided by your mental health provider, such as medication management, additional assessments, or support group participation. Take an active role in your treatment and be willing to make changes or adjustments as needed to support your recovery.

You should monitor your progress in therapy and be open to feedback from your provider about your treatment goals and progress. Be proactive in discussing any concerns or challenges that arise during treatment and work together with your provider to make adjustments as needed.

Prioritize self-care and engage in activities that promote physical, mental, and emotional well-being outside of therapy. Practice self-compassion and be patient with yourself as you navigate the ups and downs of the therapeutic process.

Seeking professional help is a positive step towards healing and recovery, and you deserve support and assistance in managing your mental health. Don't hesitate to reach out for help if you're struggling, and know that you're not alone on your journey towards better mental health and well-being.

Types of Therapy for Stress and Burnout

There are several types of therapy that can be effective in addressing stress and burnout. Here are some common types:

Cognitive Behavioral Therapy (CBT): CBT is a widely used and evidence-based therapy that focuses on identifying and changing negative thought patterns and behaviors. It helps individuals develop coping skills to manage stress more effectively, challenge irrational beliefs, and develop healthier ways of thinking and responding to stressors.

Mindfulness-Based Stress Reduction (MBSR): MBSR is a therapeutic approach that combines mindfulness meditation and yoga to help individuals reduce stress and improve overall well-being. It teaches techniques for cultivating present-moment awareness, acceptance of thoughts and emotions, and non-judgmental observation of experiences.

Acceptance and Commitment Therapy (ACT): ACT is a mindfulness-based therapy that helps individuals develop psychological flexibility by accepting difficult thoughts and emotions and committing to values-based actions. It teaches skills for mindfulness, cognitive defusion, acceptance, and values clarification to help individuals create a rich and meaningful life despite stressors.

Dialectical Behavior Therapy (DBT): DBT is a type of therapy originally developed for the treatment of borderline personality disorder but has been adapted to address various mental health concerns, including stress and burnout.
It focuses on teaching skills for emotion regulation, distress tolerance, interpersonal effectiveness, and mindfulness to help individuals cope with stressors and improve relationships.

Solution-Focused Brief Therapy (SFBT): SFBT is a goal-oriented therapy that focuses on identifying and amplifying clients' strengths and resources to facilitate positive change.
It helps individuals set specific, achievable goals and develop strategies for problem-solving and achieving those goals, often in a relatively short period of time.

Psychodynamic Therapy: Psychodynamic therapy explores how past experiences, unconscious thoughts, and relational patterns influence current behavior and emotional well-being. It can help individuals gain insight into the underlying causes of stress and burnout, resolve unresolved conflicts, and develop healthier ways of relating to themselves and others.

Group Therapy: Group therapy provides a supportive and validating environment for individuals to share their experiences, learn from others, and develop coping skills. It can be particularly beneficial for addressing burnout in work or organizational settings by fostering peer support, validation, and skill-building.

Trauma-Informed Therapy: Trauma-informed therapy acknowledges the impact of past trauma on current stress levels and focuses on creating a safe and supportive therapeutic environment. It helps individuals process and heal from traumatic experiences, develop coping skills for managing stress triggers, and build resilience.

These are just a few examples of the types of therapy that can be helpful in addressing stress and burnout. The most effective type of therapy for an individual will depend on their specific needs, preferences, and goals for treatment. It's important to work with a qualified mental health professional to determine the best approach for addressing stress and burnout.

Conclusion

Preventing burnout requires a proactive approach to managing stress, prioritizing self-care, and fostering resilience. Identify sources of stress in your life and develop coping strategies to manage them effectively, such as time management, problem-solving, or seeking social support.

Implement strategies to recognize, address, and mitigate the effects of burnout, so you can protect your well-being and maintain a healthy work-life balance. Make time for leisure activities, hobbies, and self-care practices that bring you joy and help you recharge.

Cultivate an attitude of gratitude and mindfulness in all areas of your life, bringing awareness and appreciation to each moment and experience. It's essential to prioritize self-awareness, set boundaries, seek support, and cultivate coping skills to prevent burnout from taking a toll on mental, emotional, and physical health.

Additionally, practicing mindfulness, gratitude, and positive thinking can help individuals cultivate resilience and develop a more balanced perspective on life's challenges. It is important to keep in mind that reaching out for professional assistance demonstrates strength rather than weakness. Seeking help can offer valuable support and guidance in managing burnout and enhancing overall well-being.

By incorporating these strategies into daily life and making self-care a priority, individuals can create a sustainable approach to managing stress and preventing burnout in the long term. Ultimately, prioritizing self-care and well-being is essential for maintaining health, happiness, and fulfillment in both personal and professional life.

Recap of Key Points
- Be aware of the signs and symptoms of burnout, such as exhaustion, cynicism, and decreased effectiveness.
- Establish clear boundaries between work and personal life to prevent burnout from spreading into other areas of life.
- Make self-care a priority by engaging in activities that promote physical, mental, and emotional well-being.

- Don't hesitate to reach out for help and support from friends, family, or mental health professionals when needed.
- Develop coping skills and resilience to better manage stress and bounce back from challenges.
- Incorporate mindfulness techniques into your daily routine to reduce stress and increase present-moment awareness.
- Foster gratitude by focusing on the positive aspects of life and expressing appreciation for the things you have.
- Develop a positive mindset by confronting pessimistic thoughts and directing your attention towards finding solutions instead of dwelling on problems.
- It is important to regularly evaluate your overall well-being and make necessary changes to your self-care routine.
- If burnout becomes overwhelming or persistent, don't hesitate to seek professional help from a therapist or counselor.

By implementing these key points into your life, you can effectively prevent burnout and maintain a healthy balance between work, personal life, and well-being.

Additional Resources

Here are some additional resources that may be helpful for preventing burnout and promoting well-being:

Books

- "Burnout: The Secret to Unlocking the Stress Cycle" by Emily Nagoski and Amelia Nagoski
- "Dare to Lead: Brave Work. Tough Conversations. Whole Hearts." by Brené Brown

Websites and Online Resources

- https://www.ncbi.nlm.nih.gov/pmc/articles/PMC9904840/
- https://www.nimh.nih.gov/health/statistics/any-anxiety-disorder
- https://apastyle.apa.org/products/publication-manual-7th-edition
- The American Institute of Stress https://www.stress.org/
- The World Health Organization https://www.who.int/
- https://www.mindful.org/

Apps

- Calm: Provides guided meditations, breathing exercises, and sleep stories to help reduce anxiety and improve sleep quality.

- Insight Timer: Offers a large collection of free guided meditations, music tracks, and talks on mindfulness and relaxation.

Podcasts

- "The Happiness Lab with Dr. Laurie Santos": Explores the science of happiness and provides practical tips for improving well-being.
- "The Mindful Kind": Offers mindfulness tips and exercises to help listeners incorporate mindfulness into their daily lives.

Support Groups

- Consider joining a support group or community organization focused on stress management, mental health, or well-being.
- Websites like Meetup.com or local community centers may offer support groups or meetups focused on these topics.

Bonus: Stress Diary

STRESS DIARY

I WOKE UP FEELING

Awesome   Good   Okay   Not good   Horrible

What do you want to accomplish today?

How do you want to feel today?

Today's affirmation:

Dear diary...

DATE ________

Describe a recent situation or event that caused you stress.

____

____

____

____

____

____

How did you initially react to the stressful situation?

____

____

____

____

____

____

____

What physical symptoms did you experience
when feeling stressed (e.g., headaches,
muscle tension, rapid heartbeat)?

What emotions did you experience during the
stressful situation (e.g., anxiety, frustration, anger)?

Did you notice any patterns or triggers that contributed to your stress?

____

____

____

____

____

____

What strategies have you used in the past to manage stress effectively?

____

____

____

____

____

____

____

____

What thoughts were going through your
mind when you felt stressed?

____

____

____

____

____

____

How did you cope with the stress at the moment
(e.g., deep breathing, taking a break, talking to
someone)?

____

____

____

____

____

____

____

Did you reach out for support from friends, family, or colleagues during the stressful situation?

____

____

____

____

____

____

Did engaging in any activities or hobbies help alleviate your stress?

____

____

____

____

____

____

____

Reflect on how you felt after the stressful situation had passed. Did your stress levels decrease, and if so, what contributed to this?

____

____

____

____

____

____

How would you rate your overall stress level on a scale of 1 to 10 during the day?

____

____

____

____

____

____

____

What are some positive affirmations
or self-talk statements you can use
to manage stress more effectively in
the future?

Additional Notes